FOOTBALL SUPERSTARS

by Mark and Solomon Shulman

Stride
An Imprint of The Child's World®
childsworld.com

The Child's World
childsworld.com

Published by The Child's World®
800-599-READ • www.childsworld.com

Photography Credits
Cover, 1: Focus on Football (2).
Interior: AP Images: Phelan M. Ebenhack 7; Jose Yau/Waco Tribune-Herald 28. Focus on Football: 6, 8, 10, 12, 13, 15, 16, 18, 20, 21, 23, 25, 26, 27 (2), 29. Newscom: Brian Rothmuller/Icon Sportswire DHZ 5; Debby Wong/Zuma Press 9; John Angelillo/UPI 11; K.C. Alfred/Zuma Press 17; Image of Sport 19; Michael Johnson/ZUMA Press 22.

ISBN Information
9781503858152 (Reinforced Library Binding)
9781503860728 (Portable Document Format)
9781503862081 (Online Multi-user eBook)
9781503863446 (Electronic Publication)

LCCN 2021952365

Printed in the United States of America

BRINGING THE WORLD TO YOUNG READERS 1968

FOOTBALL SUPERSTARS

TABLE OF CONTENTS

CHAPTER 1

QUARTERBACKS

Do you love football? You're not alone! More Americans watch the National Football League (NFL) than any other **pro** sports league. Even better, the Super Bowl is the most-watched sports event every year.

Most people have a favorite football team. And you probably have a different reason for liking it! Sometimes it's your hometown team, and sometimes it's the team of your favorite fans. Or maybe you just like a team's colors! It doesn't matter. In this book, you'll get to know some of today's best teams and players.

First up: the quarterbacks. They're the leaders of their team. They work with coaches to call the shots whenever they're on the field. Sometimes they pass the ball to a receiver. Sometimes they give the ball to a running back. Sometimes the quarterback runs with the ball himself!

Every play starts with the QB at the line. Here's Matthew Stafford leading the Los Angeles Rams in Super Bowl LVI.

But always, quarterbacks have one job to do, and that's to score points for their team.

Quarterbacks get most of the glory when their team wins. Or most of the blame when their team loses. No matter what, they're most fans' favorite players.

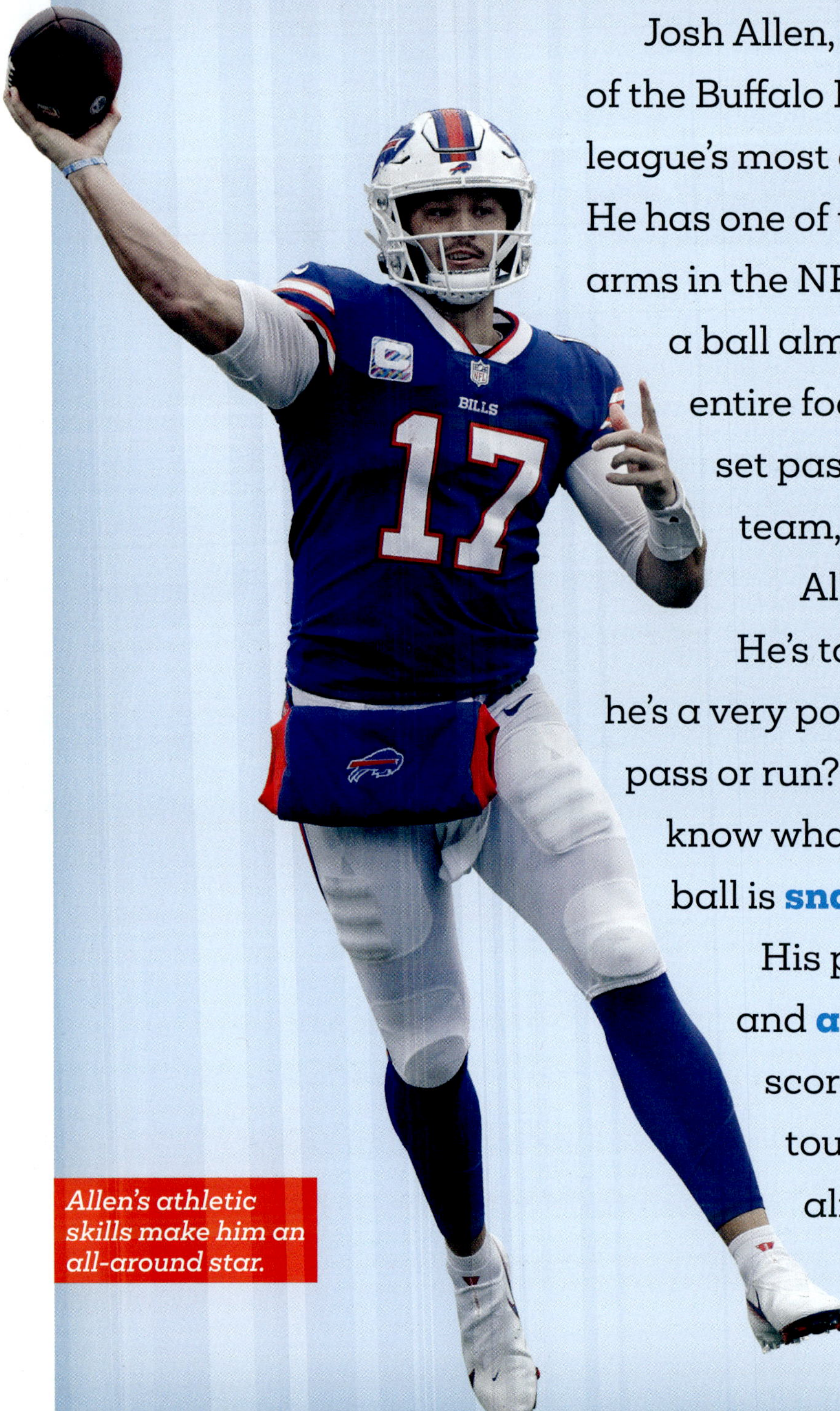

Allen's athletic skills make him an all-around star.

Josh Allen, the star quarterback of the Buffalo Bills, is among the league's most exciting players. He has one of the most powerful arms in the NFL, and can throw a ball almost as far as an entire football field. He has set passing records with his team, and the NFL, too.

Allen has many talents. He's tall and strong, and he's a very powerful runner. Will he pass or run? Other teams don't know what he'll do when the ball is **snapped**.

His passing is fast and **accurate**, and he scores more running touchdowns than almost any other quarterback.

HEARING ECHOES

In 2021, Josh Allen became the only quarterback in NFL history to get **sacked** by a defensive player with the same name: Josh Allen of the Jacksonville Jaguars! We're not joshing!

No wonder the Bills have won so many games with Allen in charge. In 2020, the multi-talented Allen led the Bills to their first AFC Championship Game in 27 years.

Lamar Jackson looks for room to run on another trip to the end zone.

Baltimore Ravens quarterback Lamar Jackson is a threat to any defense. He's a mighty passer who can move the ball downfield with his strong, accurate throws.

Lamar is also as fast as any running back, and just as tough to tackle. When defenders come to get him, Lamar can **juke** them for extra yards.

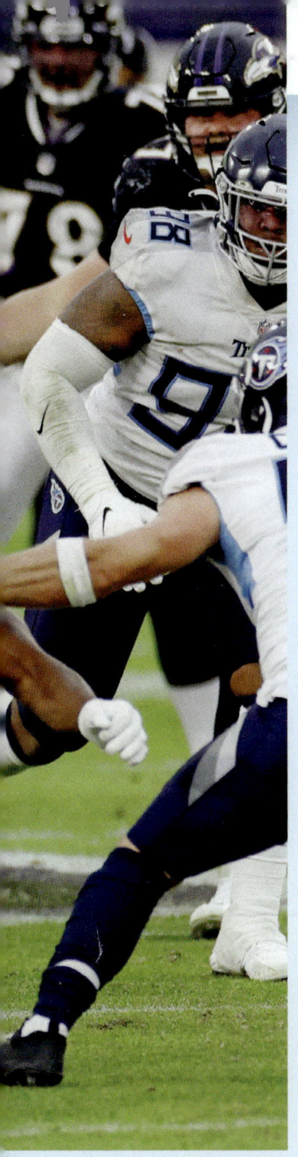

In 2019, Lamar rushed for 1,206 yards. That's the all-time NFL rushing record for any quarterback in a single season!

Lamar started his career with a bang. At just 19, he became the youngest player ever to win the Heisman Trophy. Three years later, in 2019, he was voted NFL Most Valuable Player (MVP). He's just the ninth player to have won both awards.

Every year, the Heisman goes to the top college player in the country.

The Kansas City Chiefs' Patrick Mahomes took the NFL by storm. A fast runner with a bullet-like pass, Mahomes rarely stays in the **pocket**. Defenders try to catch him, but just before he gets sacked he often makes a surprise throw for another first down!

In 2018, his first year as the **starter**, Mahomes set an NFL record as the youngest passer to throw 50 touchdown passes. The next season, Mahomes led the Chiefs to the NFL championship! Mahomes was named the Super Bowl MVP! He and the Chiefs played in the Super Bowl again in 2020, but lost to the Tampa Bay Buccaneers.

Mahomes has a strong arm and can throw from any angle.

Stafford had three TD passes in the Rams' Super Bowl win.

Matthew Stafford is a **veteran** QB known for his **clutch** plays. After 12 years with the Detroit Lions, he joined the LA Rams. With his accurate throwing and steady leadership, Stafford pushed the Rams to a Super Bowl LVI victory.

Who's next? Keep an eye on young Justin Herbert of the LA Chargers. He's got a rocket arm and he's a powerful runner. In his **rookie** year of 2020, he threw for an impressive 31 touchdowns. He added 38 more in 2021. He's just getting better!

Quarterback is the most important position in America's biggest sport. And one player is the greatest QB ever. Tom Brady has led his teams to seven Super Bowl championships. He won six with the New England Patriots and one with the Tampa Bay Buccaneers. Brady was the Super Bowl MVP five times!

It's more than just championships. Brady is the NFL's all-time leader in touchdown passes with 624. His total of passing yards, 84,520, is also the highest ever.

Brady is great at calling plays at the line.

Plus, Brady is still going strong at the age of 45. That makes him one of the oldest players ever! Brady works hard to keep his body in shape. He doesn't even eat sugar.

His teammates praise him for his leadership. No matter what the score, he stays cool and collected. One of his best games was Super Bowl LI. The Patriots trailed 28-3 in the fourth quarter. Brady led drive after drive to tie the score. In the first-ever overtime Super Bowl, Brady and the Patriots came back to beat the Atlanta Falcons, 34-28.

In NFL history, Tom Brady is the GOAT: The Greatest of All Time.

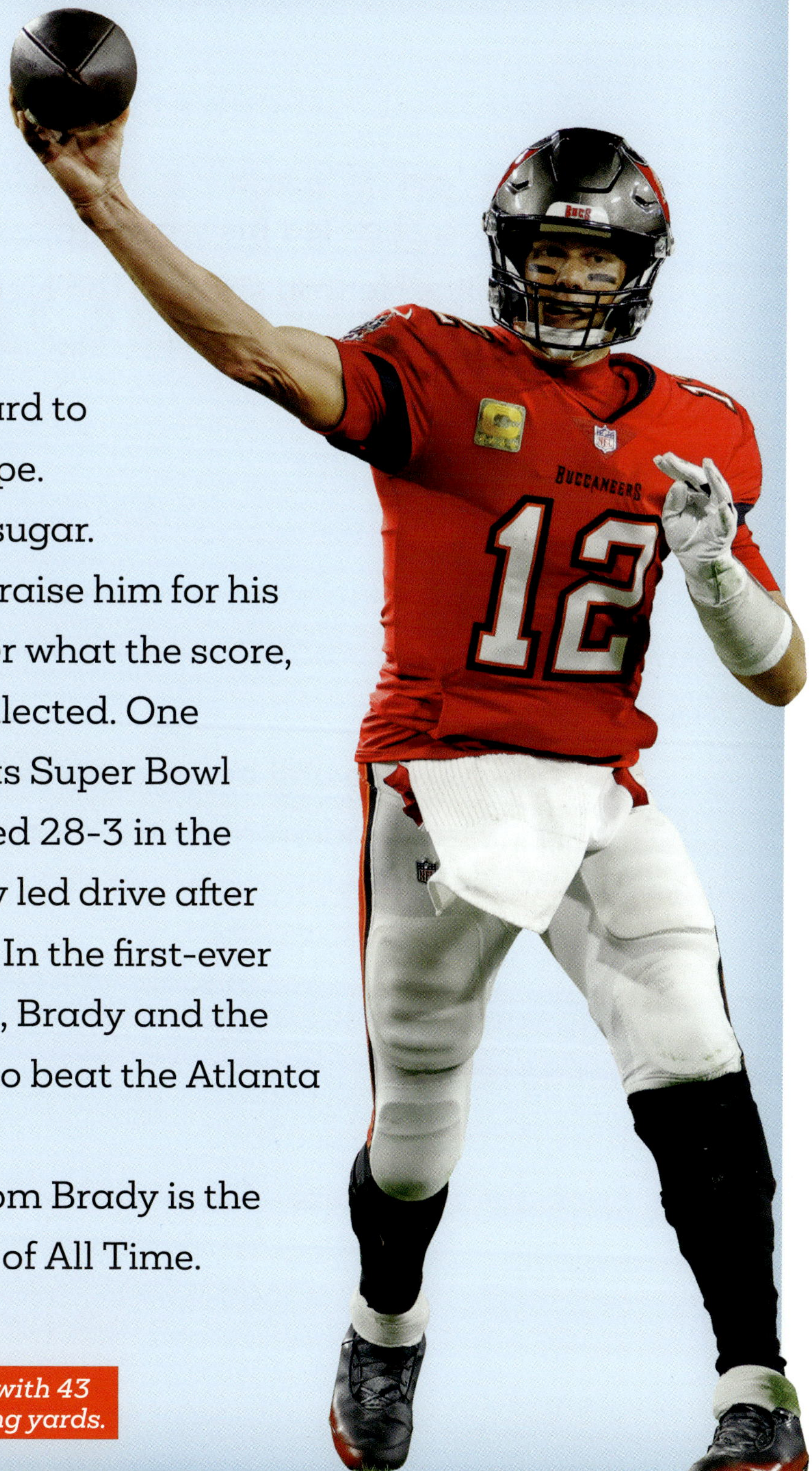

In 2021, Brady led the NFL with 43 TD passes and 5,316 passing yards.

CHAPTER 2

LIGHT UP THE SCOREBOARD!

There are three main ways to score in football. You can kick a **field goal**, catch a pass in the end zone, or run the ball for a touchdown.

Nobody runs the ball better than Derrick Henry. With his powerful legs and breakaway speed, this Tennessee Titans running back stays ahead of defenders. In 2019 and 2020, Henry led the NFL in rushing touchdowns and total rushing yards. His 2020 season was one of the best ever for a running back. Henry gained 2,072 yards, the fifth-most all-time for a single season.

Look out, defenders—Henry is a rumbling, one-man stampede!

Derrick Henry has run for more than 200 yards in five different games.

Taylor is the first Colts player to lead the NFL in rushing since 2000.

A new running superstar busted out in 2021. In his second season with the Indianapolis Colts, Jonathan Taylor had a monster year. He led the NFL in rushing yards (1,811), rushing TDs (18), and carries (331). He had 10 games with 100 or more yards. In five of those, he topped 140 yards!

Though less than six feet (1.8 m) tall, Taylor is powerful and fast. All season long, he got better and better at finding **holes** in the defense. Keep an eye on this rising star!

Another breakout star was wide receiver Cooper Kupp of the Los Angeles Rams. He was a good player for his first four seasons, but emerged in 2021 as one of the best. Kupp led the NFL with 145 catches, 16 touchdown catches, and 1,947 receiving yards. He was only the fourth player to do that in a single season. He teamed with Rams QB Matthew Stafford for big play after big play.

Kupp capped off his great season by helping the Rams win Super Bowl LVI, 23-20 over the Cincinnati Bengals. Kupp caught two touchdowns in the game. The second TD came with less than two minutes left, and gave the Rams the winning points. Kupp was named the Super Bowl MVP!

Kupp makes a game-winning TD catch in Super Bowl LVI.

Whoosh! What's that blur? It's Tyreek Hill. Nicknamed "Cheetah," the wide receiver has been clocked at more than 23 miles per hour (37 kph). That's one of the fastest speeds ever recorded in the NFL. Even when he's **double-teamed**, Hill catches long passes before blazing his way to a touchdown. After six seasons with Kansas City, Hill joined the Miami Dolphins in 2022.

Miami got a star! Here's one example from Hill's time with the Chiefs: With seven minutes left in Super Bowl LIV, Kansas City trailed by 10 points. They were deep in their own territory. On third and 15, Hill blazed past defenders, running 60 yards in five seconds before catching a long pass from Patrick Mahomes. The Chiefs soon scored, and ended up winning the game. Watch for the Cheetah in Miami!

Hill's great hands secure another catch for the Chiefs.

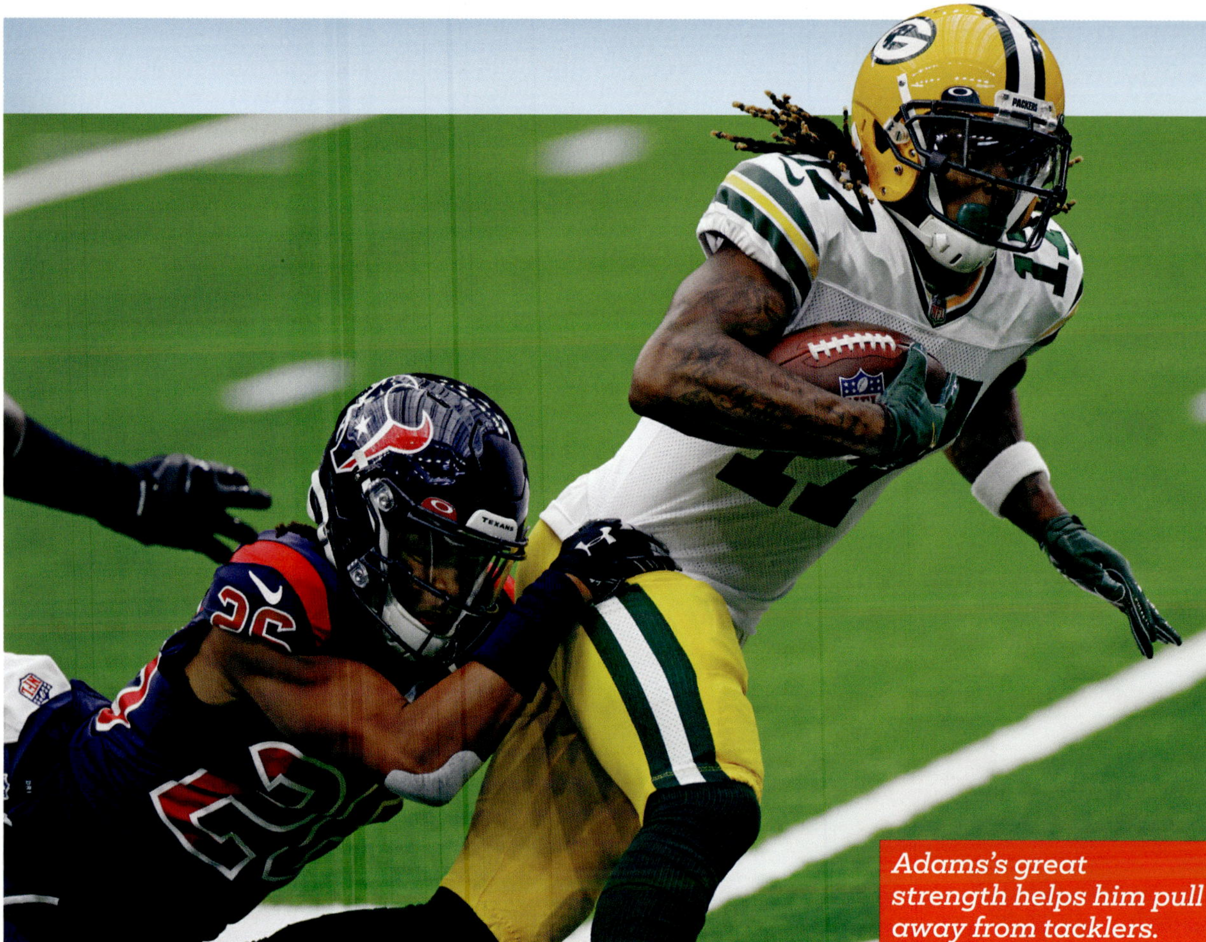

Adams's great strength helps him pull away from tacklers.

Davante Adams is another one of the NFL's best receivers. He muscles past defenders to make catch after catch. He can leap above them, too, and he has great hands. And he's so **dependable**, the quarterback can throw any pass knowing Adams will be where it lands.

In 2020, Adams led the NFL in touchdown catches with a career-best 18. He teamed with Aaron Rodgers to form one of the NFL's best offensive duos.

Adams is an all-time best, too. He has more games with 100-plus receiving yards and two touchdown catches than any other player.

When the Green Bay Packers need a last-minute, game-changing play, you'll probably see Davante Adams putting up points in the end zone!

MOVING THE CHAINS

On football sidelines, a pair of tall poles are joined together by a ten-yard chain. One pole goes where the last first down was, and the other marks where the next first down will be. Teams try to "move the chains" down the field. That means they are gaining yards and heading for the end zone.

Tight ends do lots of jobs. They act as linemen, blocking the defense. They're targets for passes. A great tight end like George Kittle can be a powerful blocker *and* a top receiver. Tall and strong, Kittle has been setting San Francisco 49ers records since he joined the team in 2017.

In one game against Philadelphia in 2020, Kittle became the first tight end in NFL history to catch at least 15 passes for at least 175 yards in a single game. He also had a team-record 210 receiving yards in a single game.

Kittle celebrates another big TD catch for the Niners.

Kittle's 1,377 receiving yards in 2018 was an NFL record until Kansas City's Travis Kelce broke it in 2020 with 1,416. Kelce is one of Patrick Mahomes's favorite targets, and helped the Chiefs win Super Bowl LIV. He was the first tight end to top 1,000 receiving yards in six straight seasons. His brother Jason is a lineman for the Philadelphia Eagles.

Kelce's height lets him soar above defenders to make big catches.

CHAPTER 3

DEFENSE! DEFENSE!

We've met the players who put the points on the board. Now let's take a look at the players who try to stop these powerful offenses. Meet the top defensive players in the NFL!

Let's start with sacks. To make a sack, you need speed, power, and toughness. In the NFL today, nobody makes sacks like Aaron Donald of the Los Angeles Rams. Watching for the moment the ball is snapped, Aaron then goes head-to-head with the offensive linemen. He can dash around them, power through them, and even pick them up and throw them aside. Then it's time to head for the passer.

Donald sacks another superstar, QB Aaron Rodgers.

Donald has been named NFL Defensive Player of the Year three times. In 2018, he led the NFL with 20.5 sacks, one of the highest single-season totals ever. In February 2022, he helped the Rams win the Super Bowl.

At the rate Donald is going, he's on pace to beat Buffalo's Bruce Smith. Smith holds the record for the most career sacks, with 201.

Another sack master is T.J. Watt of the Pittsburgh Steelers. In 2021, he became the highest-paid defensive player in history. Watt does just about everything very, very well. The hard-hitting **linebacker** was named the 2021 NFL Defensive Player of the Year. He also led the NFL in sacks in 2020 and 2021. In 2021, Watt tied the NFL's all-time record with 22.5 sacks. (How do you get half a sack? You combine with a teammate to tackle the QB.) Plus, few players can force a **fumble** as well as Watt can. He had an NFL-best eight forced fumbles in 2019.

Watt sacks Cincinnati's Joe Burrow on his way to tying an NFL record.

BROTHERS WHO BASH

T.J.'s brother J.J. was a three-time NFL Defensive Player of the Year. J.J. starred for the Houston Texans and Arizona Cardinals. Their brother Derek was also an NFL fullback. Another great pair of brothers, Nick and Joey Bosa, are both superstar defenders. Nick (left) is a defensive end for the 49ers, while Joey is a star linebacker with the Chargers. They both made the 2022 **Pro Bowl**.

Trevon Diggs must have learned how to play defensive back in his backyard. His brother Stefon has become a top wide receiver for the Buffalo Bills. Meanwhile, Trevon is now one of the NFL's top **cornerbacks**. In 2021, he led the NFL with 11 interceptions. He returned two of them for touchdowns. At one point, he had at least one "pick" in six straight games for the Dallas Cowboys.

Diggs leaps high for one of his NFL-best 11 "picks."

Tyrann Mathieu of the Chiefs first became famous in the NFL for his nickname: Honey Badger. But he quickly showed that he was worth knowing for his great skill. He spent five years with Arizona before joining the Chiefs in 2019. They won a Super Bowl that season, so perhaps he was the secret to victory! Mathieu has had at least one interception in each of his nine NFL seasons.

Miami's Xavien Howard is another star cornerback. A football website rated him No. 1 in the NFL for keeping receivers from catching the ball. Howard uses speed, quick hands, and football smarts to stay ahead of the offense.

From the first snap to the final whistle, NFL players do their best to win. The players in this book have done more than their share. Who is your favorite?

Howard's teammates celebrate after he makes an interception.

GLOSSARY

accurate (AK-yer-ut) very precise in hitting a target by passing

clutch (KLUTCH) able to succeed when a team needs it most

cornerbacks (KOR-ner-bax) defensive football players who cover opposing wide receivers

dependable (dih-PEN-duh-buhl) trustworthy and reliable

double-teamed (DUB-ul-TEEMD) when a player on offense is covered by a pair of defenders

field goal (FEELD GOHL) a placekick that goes over the crossbar and between the uprights, worth three points

fumble (FUM-bull) when a player carrying the ball drops it on the field

holes (HOHLZ) spaces between offensive lineman

juke (JOOK) fool or confuse a defender while running

linebacker (LYN-bak-er) a defensive player who sets up behind the line of scrimmage

pocket (PAH-ket) the area formed by blockers around the quarterback

pro (PRO) paid to play sports; short for professional

Pro Bowl (PRO BOWL) the NFL's annual all-star game, played right before the Super Bowl

rookie (RUH-kee) a player in his first season as a pro

sacked (SAKT) when the quarterback is tackled for a loss

snapped (SNAPT) handed or tossed the football to the quarterback to start a play

starter (START-er) a player who begins the game on the field

veteran (VET-er-en) in sports, a player who has played several pro seasons

THINK ABOUT IT

Who was your favorite player in this book? Explain your answer.

What is your favorite NFL team? Why?

If you could play any position in football, which would you choose? Why?

FIND OUT MORE

IN THE LIBRARY

Davidson, B. Keith. *NFL*. New York, NY: Crabtree Publishing, 2022.

Kelley, K.C. *Top 10 Quarterbacks*. Mankato, MN: The Child's World, 2019.

Lowe, Alexander. *G.O.A.T. Football Running Backs*. Minneapolis, MN: Lerner Publications, 2023.

ON THE WEB

Visit our website for links about the NFL:
childsworld.com/links

Note to Parents, Teachers, and Librarians: We routinely verify our Web links to make sure they are safe and active sites. So encourage your readers to check them out!

INDEX

ABOUT THE AUTHORS

MARK AND SOLOMON SHULMAN have teamed up to write several books on pro sports, including a history of the Kansas City Chiefs. They especially enjoyed writing a book about their favorite team, the Buffalo Bills. Mark is also the author of dozens of other nonfiction books for kids. The Shulmans live in New York City.